UCHE DAVID UCHE

MoneyTips

20 powerful tips for business, career & financial success

First published by Uche David Uche 2019

Copyright © 2019 by Uche David Uche

All rights reserved. No part of this publication may be reproduced, stored or transmitted in any form or by any means, electronic, mechanical, photocopying, recording, scanning, or otherwise without written permission from the publisher. It is illegal to copy this book, post it to a website, or distribute it by any other means without permission.

Uche David Uche asserts the moral right to be identified as the author of this work.

While every precaution has been taken in the preparation of this book, the publisher assumes no responsibility for errors or omissions, or for damages resulting from the use of the information contained herein.

Email: uche@uchedaviduche.com

First edition

This book was professionally typeset on Reedsy.
Find out more at reedsy.com

Dedication

*To my family,
for their love, support and sacrifice.*

Contents

Preface	ii
Keep your money lines open	1
Let your talents determine your career	2
Make productive use of time	3
Identify your target market	4
Operate as a team	5
Let the packaging enhance sales	6
Build your customer base	7
Follow due process	8
Listen to good music	9
Don't spend it all	10
Be careful who you associate with	11
Protect your assets	12
Think Generationally	13
Develop people skills	14
Treat your customers well	15
Give some freebies	16
Think about owning a business	17
Start on a smaller scale	18
Pay attention to your customer	19
Be systematic about it	20
About the Author	21

Preface

MoneyTips is a series of short, inspiring and helpful financial advice. It provides quick and effective solutions to business, career and financial issues.

MoneyTips will help you to excel in your work or business and make good money.

In this collection, you will find twenty (20) powerful tips on various areas of your work, business and financial matters.

Every tip is clear, insightful and skillfully delivered.

You will enjoy this book!

Cheers!

Uche David Uche

1

Keep your money lines open

It is through people and relationships that money flows. So, relationships are money lines. Money may stop flowing or increasing if relationships are strained, weakened or broken. Keep your money lines open. Cultivate and strengthen helpful family, business, banking, professional, social and spiritual relationships.

2

Let your talents determine your career

You will be more passionate, productive and fulfilled if your career is shaped by your talents, gifts or innate abilities. Let your talents determine your career, no matter your education or qualification(s). Find out what your key talent(s) are and let them define and enrich you.

3

Make productive use of time

Your time at work should really count for you and your company. Don't use office hours in such a way that you end up without money, returns or results. Time is perishable, so make prudent and productive use of it. Focus on the things that are important and helpful in achieving your work or business goals.

4

Identify your target market

You cannot sell to everyone profitably. Neither can you serve everyone at once. You need to identify the right group of customers to focus on. To identify your target market, you ought to do some brainstorming and market research.

5

Operate as a team

Don't work alone or run your company like its success depends on you alone. Don't limit the strength and fortunes of your company. Operate in the power of the collective. Communicate, collaborate and carry your team along in whatever you're doing. Operate as a team and see your business grow.

6

Let the packaging enhance sales

People see the packaging before the product. Let the packaging of your product indicate and enhance its value. Let the packaging be appropriate, attractive and persuasive. Let the packaging help to convince customers to buy from you.

7

Build your customer base

Don't invest heavily in an office before creating or enlarging your customer base. Don't spend money you can't recoup. Build your customer base. Define your target customers and determine how best to win and retain them. The real evidence that you are in business is that you have customers and they are paying.

8

Follow due process

Don't avoid or violate due process. Process is protective and profitable. Process prevents errors, damages and losses, including financial losses. Find out and follow established guidelines, procedures, rules or policies. It will make you more reliable, respectable and successful in your business and financial endeavors.

9

Listen to good music

What you have to offer in exchange for money is right inside you. What you have to do to create wealth is within your capacity. Unlock your potentials, hidden ideas and creative abilities with good and inspiring music.

10

Don't spend it all

Don't spend all your income or inheritance, no matter how huge. You will need money today, tomorrow and the day after. You will need the security that money brings. Secure your future. Save and invest a part of your money.

11

Be careful who you associate with

The success and stability of a business, project or venture is determined to a great extent by the people involved. Be careful who you associate or do business with. Seek and associate with people that are credible, capable and committed to you or your cause (e.g. vision, ideas, values).

12

Protect your assets

To avoid losses and unhappiness, protect your money. Protect your money and the relationships, work, business or investments that bring you money. Protect these assets by being watchful, knowledgeable and prudent in handling them.

13

Think Generationally

Your company can continue after you retire or die. Its products or services can continue to benefit society. Think generationally and put a succession plan in place. Let your wealth be preserved for future generations.

14

Develop people skills

Money is found in the hands of people, through people and for the use of people. Learn how to relate with people. Learn how to carry people along and achieve your business, career and financial goals. Learn how to win and keep customers.

15

Treat your customers well

People will buy and keep buying from a seller who treats them well. Be friendly with your customers and create a lasting relationship with them. Be attentive to their needs and responsive to their complaints. Treat them as very important people.

16

Give some freebies

Don't start out by charging for all your products or services. Give out some free products as a promotional or goodwill gesture. Give to customers, financiers, partners and others. People appreciate freebies. Use freebies to build important business relationships.

17

Think about owning a business

If you get fired or retire you can't transfer or bequeath your job to your family. Think about starting, buying or investing in a business. Business owners earn more than employees. Business owners don't get fired. Business owners can bequeath their businesses or transfer their shareholding to their family and loved ones.

18

Start on a smaller scale

Starting a business on a large scale is costly and risky. If things go wrong or your business fails, you will lose a lot. Start on a smaller scale and grow your business into the size you desire or envision. Start at a level you have good capacity for and are more secure.

19

Pay attention to your customer

Pay attention to your customer. Your pay or profit comes through him. Observe him as he comes. Listen to him as he speaks. Get to know him and what he wants. Get to know what makes him happy and what doesn't.

20

Be systematic about it

People will enjoy doing business with you if you are organized and focused. Be systematic. Establish procedures and standards for every area of your business. With good systems in place, you will be more effective as a leader, your team more productive and your business more successful.

About the Author

Uche David Uche is an inspiring business coach, chartered accountant and author. He likes to make life easier for people and help them grow their businesses, companies and careers.

Uche is passionate about providing guidance and helping entrepreneurs to grow their businesses in an easier and more fulfilling manner.

You can book or contact him as follows: uche@uche-daviduche.com or uchechukwudaviduche@gmail.com.

You can connect with me on:
- http://www.uchedaviduche.com/
- https://twitter.com/uchedaviduche1
- https://facebook.com/UcheDavidUche21
- https://www.linkedin.com/in/uche-david-uche
- https://www.instagram.com/uchedaviduche21

Subscribe to my newsletter:
✉ http://eepurl.com/c9v1fT

www.ingramcontent.com/pod-product-compliance
Lightning Source LLC
Chambersburg PA
CBHW030600220526
45463CB00007B/3124